W9-CKI-267
GOO
#21659

Cult Awareness

Cult Awareness

A Hot Issue

David Goodnough

Enslow Publishers, Inc.

40 Industrial Road   PO Box 38
Box 398   Aldershot
Berkeley Heights, NJ 07922   Hants GU12 6BP
USA   UK

http://www.enslow.com

Copyright © 2000 by Enslow Publishers, Inc.

Library of Congress Cataloging-in-Publication Data

Goodnough, David.
    Cult awareness : a hot issue / David Goodnough.
        p. cm. — (Hot issues)
    Includes bibliographical references and index.
    Summary: Discusses issues related to cults, giving examples of various cults and how they affect society.
    ISBN 0-7660-1196-8
    1. Cults—Juvenile literature. [1. Cults.] I. Title. II. Series.
BP603.G66   2000
291—DC21   98-40423
                                      CIP
                                       AC

Printed in the United States of America

10 9 8 7 6 5 4 3 2 1

To Our Readers:
All Internet addresses in this book were active and appropriate when we went to press. Any comments or suggestions can be sent by e-mail to Comments@enslow.com or to the address on the back cover.

Contents

Chapter 1

Cults in the News

When two county sheriff's deputies received a call to go to a house in Rancho Santa Fe, twenty miles north of San Diego, California, they expected to answer only a routine request for an investigation of a missing person or pet. It was 3:00 P.M. on Wednesday, March 26, 1997. Crime and violence were practically unknown in this area of quiet roads that wound around large estates and grand houses reached only by long driveways. As they approached the mansion at 18421 Colina Norte, they had their first inkling that something was wrong. They noticed a sickly sweet smell coming from the house. When no one answered the front door, they decided to enter by the back door. What they found inside stunned them.

Thirty-nine bodies lay throughout the house, on beds and mattresses on the floor. They were all clad in black shirts and trousers with brand-new black Nike athletic shoes on their feet. There were twenty-one women and eighteen men, ranging in age from twenty-six to seventy-two. They had all died after drinking a mixture of sleeping pills and alcohol before slipping plastic bags over their heads. The medical examiner later determined that they had died in stages, fifteen at a time until there were seven left. The last two assisted the others and then took their own lives.[1] This scenario was easily figured out by examining the bodies and how they were scattered throughout the house. However, one question remained: Why?

Heaven's Gate

It soon became apparent that the men and women who had killed themselves in this methodical manner were members of a cult. A cult is usually defined as a group of people bound together by devotion to a person or an idea and which is usually religious in nature. This particular cult was named Heaven's Gate. Its members were devoted to Marshall Applewhite, a sixty-five-year-old former music professor and the son of a Presbyterian minister. Applewhite believed that he was chosen to witness the end of the world as predicted in the biblical Book of Revelations.

Applewhite also believed in extraterrestrial travel. He claimed that the end of the world would be signaled by a visitation from outer space. The combination of the coming Christian holy season of Easter and a celestial happening—the appearance in the skies of the Hale-Bopp comet—convinced him that the end of the world was near. He therefore prepared his followers for their "departure" (suicide), so they could join a spaceship that was following the comet and be transported into the afterlife where they would eventually be reborn. The police discovered these plans from audiotapes and letters that the cult members had left behind with their

A coroner's truck is shown leaving the mansion in Rancho Santa Fe, California, where members of the Heaven's Gate cult engaged in a mass suicide.

bodies or had sent to relatives and friends before they killed themselves. In these messages, cult members expressed their willingness and happiness in their action and cheerfully anticipated their coming transportation to future glory and a higher form of life. They had also used the new medium of the Internet to reveal their intentions to the outside world. To people who keep track of cults, using the Internet was a new characteristic of cult groups.

There is nothing new about cults, however. Cults have existed throughout history. Ancient Greece had its secret societies that limited the worship of their gods to a select few who were initiated into their "mysteries." The Middle Ages had its elite bands of knights and monks who conducted their activities in secret. The eighteenth and nineteenth centuries had trade and craft groups bound together by strange signs and symbols. However, it was during the second half of the twentieth century that cults began to gain the general public's attention. This occurred mostly because of the attention given to cults by newspapers, radio, and television.

Charles Manson and His Family

The modern era of cults, or at least the public's awareness of them, began in 1969, when members of a "family" led by Charles Manson killed five people in Bel Air, California. One of the victims was a movie actress, Sharon Tate, wife of the film director Roman Polanski. The resulting publicity revealed the strange, secretive, and destructive aspects of what were formerly considered no more than harmless groups of eccentrics who chose to pursue a different mode of living and worship. Manson was a strange man with a criminal background who managed to wield hypnotic power over a small group of people who were so devoted to him that they would do anything for him, even kill at his command.

Manson convinced his followers that he was Jesus Christ and had returned to earth to bring about the end of the world. Only Manson and his family would escape the world's end through an underground tunnel. The location of this tunnel would be revealed to him—and him only—on the last day of the world. Manson hoped to hasten the end of the world by causing a racial war between blacks and whites. He would start the war by blaming the murders committed by his cult on African Americans. Manson, along with three members of his family, was found guilty of murder and put into prison where he remains to this day. A shocked nation breathed a sigh of relief, and the Manson cult soon faded from the general public's memory. However, Manson still has a few devoted followers who keep in touch with him and one another on the Internet.

The Jonestown Mass Suicide

Almost ten years later on November 18, 1978, the world was shocked by an even stranger and more horrible cult-related happening. The Reverend Jim Jones, the leader of a cult named the People's Temple, ordered the mass murder or suicide of more than nine hundred people who had settled in Jonestown, the community's headquarters in Guyana, South America. The tragedy came about because of a visit to Jonestown by Congressman Leo J. Ryan of California. Ryan was investigating charges that some of the cult members were being held captive and that children in the group were being abused. As Ryan and his party left Jonestown for the airstrip where their plane was waiting, they were ambushed by members of Jones's community. Ryan, three newsmen, and one of the cult members who had brought the charges against Jones were killed. Jones then told his followers, "If we can't live in peace, then let's die in peace."[2] A vat of Kool-Aid poisoned with cyanide was brought out, and the cult members lined up to drink from it. Apparently they had been practicing this ritual mass suicide for months and most members drank the poison willingly. Those who resisted were shot or injected with poison. A few escaped into the surrounding

*M*ore than nine hundred members of the People's Temple in Jonestown, Guyana, killed themselves in November 1978 by drinking grape punch laced with cyanide poison.

jungle. Jones either shot himself in the head or had one of his henchmen do it for him.

Other Destructive Cults

Since the Jonestown tragedy, the violent and destructive activities of cults have continued at a steady rate. In April 1993, David Koresh and seventy-three of his followers in the Branch Davidian biblical cult were burned to death in Waco, Texas, during a confrontation with federal authorities. In October 1994, fifty-three members of a Switzerland-based doomsday cult named the Order of the Solar Temple died in a murder-suicide ritual. Fourteen members of the same cult were found dead in a similar ritual in Grenoble, France, in December 1995. In Japan, members of the Aum Supreme Truth cult staged a gas attack, on the Japanese subway system in retaliation against the government, which they felt was persecuting them.[3] Twelve innocent people died in the attack, and more than four thousand were injured.

What had once seemed erratic and widely separated events became, due to the sensational publicity in the world's media, a worldwide problem. It has been estimated that there are between three thousand and five thousand cults in the United States alone.[4] Informed people, as well as concerned organizations and governments, began to ask how these groups could hold such absolute control over their members. What was the origin and history of these groups? What teaching or doctrines did they hold that could lead them to separate themselves from their fellow citizens and commit murder and suicide? Are there other, similar groups in our midst? How can they be recognized?

Chapter 2

What Is a Cult?

There are probably as many definitions of a cult as there are cults. Every special group of people sees itself as distinct and unique, whether it is the Boy Scouts or a commune of vegetarians or herbalists. In the case of cults, therefore, it is useful to begin with a dictionary definition.

Cults Defined

Most dictionaries define a cult as, first, a religious system; second, an intense devotion to a person, ideal, or thing; and, third, a group or sect bound together by that devotion.

Many people agree that there is a religious aspect to cults. However, they believe that cults by most definitions are outside the bounds of accepted world religions such as Christianity, Judaism, Islam, Hinduism, and a host of others that number their believers in the millions. To these people, cults have a negative impact. They are un-Christian or un-Islamic or un-whatever religion you believe in. In short, they are nonbelievers; they are even sinful. To those who have no religious belief, cult members are simply outsiders or strange people who won't conform. While some see them as a threat to our social system, others see them as harmless rebels.

To many other people, cults are simply new religions or merely alternatives to accepted religious beliefs. In a country such as the United States, which jealously guards its freedoms of speech, assembly, and religion, cults have every right to exist. Therefore, there is a controversy in the simple definition of a cult as a religious system.

The second part of the dictionary definition is also troublesome, because it involves devotion to a leader or to an idea or to both. Most people who have studied and written about cults agree that the most obvious thing about them is that they have a strong leader or founder who claims to have special wisdom or power. This person is able to convince others of his or her superiority. Such a leader may use influence to persuade followers to adopt attitudes or commit actions that are not considered appropriate by most people. In many cases, the followers of the leader are so devoted to him or her that they will do anything they are commanded to do. Critics of cults have charged that these leaders have gained control over their followers by mind control—sometimes called "brainwashing"—or even by hypnotism.

The third part of the definition has to do with the structure of the group. The members are bound together by their devotion to their leader, an ideal, or a thing. This devotion is so strong that they consider themselves different from people who do not feel the same way. They sometimes go to great lengths to emphasize their difference. They may wear unusual clothing or shave their heads or display symbols that only they understand. In some ways, they are similar to Christian or Buddhist monks and nuns. However, their leaders usually tell them that they are superior to other people and should associate only with one another. This further isolates them from society and the realities of everyday living.

Characteristics of Cults

Most cults have the following characteristics in common:

1. The cult has a living leader who claims to have ultimate wisdom.

2. The cult has an authoritarian power structure—that is, all power is invested in the leader.

3. The cult has rigid boundaries, which means that cult members stay within their group and shun or distrust all outsiders.[1]

All cults are different and there are many variations of these three characteristics. If we examine one of the most recent cults that has made news, Heaven's Gate, we see that it is unique in its details but similar to other cults in its broad outlines.

Heaven's Gate actually had two leaders, Marshall H. Applewhite and Bonnie Lu Nettles, who both shared an interest in the occult and reincarnation, or life after death. They were convinced that they were the only two people, or "witnesses," who understood the biblical Book of Revelations, which describes the end of the world, or the apocalypse. They formed a small group in 1975 and claimed to be extraterrestrials from a higher form of life who would lead their followers to

Types of Cults

Margaret Thaler Singer, a psychologist and professor at the University of California, Berkeley, has identified ten major types of cults. Each has its own leaders, beliefs, reasons for being, and structure but can be identified as one of the following:

1. Neo (or New)-Christian religious

2. Hindu and Eastern religious

3. Occult, witchcraft, and satanist

4. Spiritualist

5. Zen and other Chinese-Japanese mystical systems

6. Racial

7. Flying saucer and other outer-space phenomena

8. Psychological

9. Political

10. Self-help, self-improvement, and lifestyle (New Age)

Source: Margaret Thaler Singer with Janja Lalich, *Cults in Our Midst* (San Francisco: Jossey-Bass Publishers, 1995).

a new life after the apocalypse. Nettles died in 1985, and Applewhite and his small group went underground. They resurfaced in 1992 and began to recruit new members through television advertisements and the Internet.

Here we have a leader who claimed absolute wisdom on the subject of death and reincarnation. He was able to attract and retain followers who were willing to devote themselves to him and his ideas. In the early 1990s, Applewhite and the cult members rented a mansion in Rancho Santa Fe, north of San Diego. The community was very tolerant, and the longtime residents knew that their new neighbors were involved in some sort of religious activity. However, no one was interested or concerned enough to investigate what it was. The "monks," as the neighbors called the cult members,

Students in Cults

✓ Were students when they joined the cult 43%

✓ Were high school students....................... 10%

✓ Were college students 27%

✓ Were graduate students......................... 6%

✓ Dropped out of school after joining cult........ 38%

Source: Preliminary report on the "Questionnaire for Former Members of Charismatic Groups," prepared by Michael D. Langone, Ph.D., for *Cultic Studies Journal*, American Family Foundation, Bonita Springs, FL 34133, July 20, 1992.

"were dressed in black pajamas, like Viet Cong."[2] They believed that

> Their bodies were mere vessels. By renouncing sex, drugs, alcohol, their birth names and all relationships with family and friends, disciples could become ready to ascend to space, shedding their "containers," or bodies, and entering God's Kingdom.

They worked at computers, sending their message through the Internet, and had their own Web site. They even created their own Web design company, Higher Source, which designed Web pages for many clients in the southern California area. Here was a highly structured community, entirely devoted to a leader and his idea of deliverance from this world to a privileged existence in another world.

Many people who believe that cults are no more than alternative forms of religion point out that all of the characteristics of modern cults are exactly those of early religious sects, most notably Christianity.[3] This is no doubt true, but with one important difference: Christianity, as well as Judaism, Islam, Buddhism, Mormonism, Jehovah's Witnesses, Seventh Day Adventists, and all other established movements or sects within those religions, did not self-destruct. They entered the mainstream of human life and tried to improve that life.

Chapter 3

Where Do Cults Come From?

Cults are not particular to one century or country. They have been present since the beginning of recorded history. They probably existed before that since prehistoric tribes and clans were dependent on a strong leader who probably claimed that his power came from whatever gods the group worshiped.

More than two thousand years ago, the Greek philosopher and mathematician Pythagoras founded a school that sounds more like a cult than an institution for learning. Pythagoras taught his students that mathematics could provide them with all they needed to know about anything. This included even God, whom he called the One. He also believed in past lives. He was a strict vegetarian and urged his students to follow his example. He told them that if they abstained from all pleasures and lived pure lives, their souls would become godlike. His students adored him and believed that he had magical or superhuman powers. Some people claimed that he could appear in two places at once. They also believed that he could perform many other miracles, such as taming wild animals by whispering in their ears.[1]

Cults can appear or be formed at any time, but most seem to be formed during times of major changes or events such as war, famine, plague, political and social upheavals, or radical alterations in the way people live.[2] The twentieth century, for example, has seen incredible changes in transportation, communication, and the structure of society that would have been unbelievable to people living in previous centuries. Perhaps this could explain the rise of so many cults in our time. Some people became so overwhelmed by the exploding technology that has transformed their lives that they turned to anyone who preached a simpler way of life and declared that he or she had the wisdom and the means to achieve it.

Cult Formation

The usual first step in the formation of a cult is for a single person to announce that he or she knows the truth of existence and has a mission to bring it to a select chosen few. Of course, there are variations of this—sometimes there may be two people—but the pattern is almost always the same. How this leader has achieved his superior knowledge varies widely. It could come about through visions, dreams, drugs, and even from being captured by extraterrestrials and taken to some other planet for instruction.

Whatever the source of their knowledge or power, these leaders must be strong-willed, persuasive, and completely self-centered. They remain at the top of whatever structure the cult takes, and all authority and decision making rests with them. They also are the center of attention for cult members. All love, respect, devotion, or veneration of the cult members is directed toward *them*. If any rivals emerge, they are expelled from the cult. Many leaders of cults are so obsessed with personal control that they demand extreme sacrifices from their followers, such as giving up all their possessions, their jobs and careers, and even their children. These sacrifices by members, incidentally, become the main source of income for the cults and their leaders. Many of the leaders lead lavish lifestyles, all based on the financial sacrifices made by their followers.

To the average person, this would seem to be one gigantic fraud. One would have to be incredibly naive

*B*egun as a cult during a time of spiritual turmoil, Islam is now a major world religion. Here, Muslim believers pray at Mecca, the birthplace of the prophet Mohammed and the holiest site of Islam.

to sign over his or her life's savings to somebody who claimed to have been taken up in a flying saucer and taught the universe's secrets by a superior race that had populated the earth millions of years ago. But thousands of people have done exactly that.

Cults and Religions

Most of the major religions began as cults during times of great change. Christianity, for example, began during the breakup of the Roman Empire and flourished during the Dark and Middle Ages. Mohammad, the prophet of Islam, lived in a time of spiritual turmoil. He was forced to wage war throughout his life to achieve the spiritual life for his followers, which had been revealed to him in visions. Moses, who according to the Old Testament spoke directly to God, led his people out of slavery in Egypt. Likewise, the breakup of Russian communism in Eastern Europe at the end of the twentieth century has left many people confused, resentful, and despairing and has begun to produce many cults and alternative religions.[3] Whether any of them will take hold remains to be seen, but the conditions for their growth, if not their success, are there.

Cults such as those that have led to the great religions and to benevolent organizations, such as Freemasons or Jehovah's Witnesses, have been in many ways beneficial to and influential in our culture and society. But it cannot be denied that many—some would say most—cults have been destructive or even, as in the case of the Manson cult, evil.

Chapter 4

What Kinds of Cults Are There?

A cult can be formed around any person, ideal, or thing. All that is required is a persuasive leader and persuaded followers. There are personality cults, such as those that are devoted to deceased celebrities who are believed to be still alive by their followers through sightings, visions, and dreams. There are cults based on ideals, such as the ones that have grown up around the New Age movement with its emphasis on a simple lifestyle, a pure environment, and physical well-being. There are cults based on things, such as curious land formations that resemble beasts or humans.

Apocalyptic Cults

The most familiar cults are religious cults, usually Christian in belief and based on different inter-pretations of the Bible. The last book of the New Testament, the Book of Revelations, has proved to be the inspiration for untold numbers of cults, since it deals with the end of the world—the apocalypse—and the triumph of good over evil in a last great battle. Doomsday, or apocalyptic, cults generally believe that the world will soon end and that they alone will survive and live forever in an earthly or cosmic paradise. These cults take many forms and have widely differing versions of the apocalypse. The Manson cult, for example, believed that the final great battle would be a racial war between blacks and whites.

A less destructive doomsday cult, and one that is familiar to most people, is Jehovah's Witnesses. Its members believe that the world's end is coming on a certain date. They prepare for it by praying and leading what they believe to be exemplary lives— they are strongly opposed to war and violence, for instance. They used to announce specific dates for the end of the world, and when these dates came around and nothing happened, they would simply announce a new date and go about their business, awaiting the final day. They have been in existence since 1870 and have a worldwide membership of more than 4 million, so most people consider them no longer a cult but a sect or offshoot of Christianity.

Most doomsday cults are destructive, however, and try to hasten the final day. Their members usually gather together in communes or isolated structures and prepare to defend themselves in the coming final battle. The reason the Branch Davidians of Waco, Texas, attracted the attention of the authorities is that they had armed themselves with an arsenal of weapons. In 1989 a cult headed by Jeffrey Lundgren in Kirtland, Ohio, murdered five of its members. The reason? Lundgren said he had found coded messages in the Bible that told him that the end of the world was coming. Lundgren and his fellow members, fifteen in all, decided to

Charles Manson, who is serving time in San Quentin Prison in California, was denied parole in 1997 for the ninth time.

murder a whole family as sacrifices to entice Jesus Christ back to earth to start the apocalypse.

Many leaders of cults claim to be the Messiah or the Second Christ. Others base their wisdom and power on visions of heaven or another cosmic world. Indeed, many cults register themselves with state governments as nonprofit organizations or churches. They may even request that they be excused from paying taxes. The Church of Scientology, for example, has all the characteristics of a cult and yet has set itself up as a legitimate religious institution.

The Unification Church

Another very successful cult that has set itself up as a legitimate religion is the Unification Church, founded and headed by Sun Myung Moon. Moon is a Korean whose parents had converted to Christianity. He attended services of the Presbyterian Church and was very moved by the life and sorrows of Jesus. He claims that at the age of sixteen he had a vision of Jesus who told him that his work on earth had never been completed and that he had chosen Moon to finish that work and establish his kingdom on earth.

Moon established his church in 1948 in North Korea and began to travel throughout the country to preach and gain followers. North Korea was a Communist country that did not allow religious freedom. The authorities accused Moon of attempting to overthrow the government and arrested him several times. He continued preaching and writing and managed to gain a large group of loyal followers. By the 1960s he was successful enough to send missionaries to other countries, including the United States. He made world tours,

*R*everend Moon and his wife wave to more than forty thousand people attending a mass-wedding ceremony in Seoul, South Korea, on August 25, 1992.

preaching against communism and spreading his message that he was chosen by Jesus to purify mankind. In 1972 he claimed to have had a revelation that directed him to emigrate to the United States. He then began an all-out campaign to gain more followers by holding huge revival meetings in cities across the country.

Moon attracted many new followers, or "Moonies" as they were called, who raised funds for the church by selling candies and herbs door-to-door and in airports and railroad stations, just as the Hare Krishnas (members of another cult) had done. He began to import an oriental root called ginseng, which proved very popular in the health food industry. He also invested in real estate and other money-making ventures. Eventually he amassed a fortune estimated at more than $200 million.

Like many other cult leaders, Moon led a very expensive and lavish life, and it soon got him into trouble with the Internal Revenue Service. In 1984 he was convicted of tax evasion and was jailed for eighteen months. He still has loyal followers, but the membership of his church has dwindled to an estimated six thousand followers.[1]

Non-Christian Religious Cults

There are many religious cults that claim to be entirely independent of any established religion. They refer to themselves as emerging faith groups. Wicca is an emerging faith group whose beliefs are derived from ancient pagan beliefs and practices of northern Europe. As its name implies, it practices a new form of witchcraft. There has always been an interest in witchcraft, and it has become a part of literature, music, and art. One of the first to actually practice witchcraft in the modern era was Gerald B. Gardner, a British civil service employee. He published a book of spells in 1951 and established a coven of witches who tried to revive the old rituals of witchcraft. Wicca came to the United States in the early 1960s and soon found many followers. Perhaps the best-known modern witch is Sybil Leek, who writes books, appears on television, and speaks out frequently in support of what she believes is a revival of one of the earliest religions.

Santería. Santería is a non-Christian cult that has its roots in voodoo, a magical system brought to the

Caribbean by African slaves. Santería developed in Cuba in the 1800s when voodoo followers adopted many of the practices of the Roman Catholic Church into their rituals. It spread to the United States in 1959 when Fidel Castro became dictator of Cuba and forced many Santeríans to flee their country. Santeríans believe in spirits that will make themselves known during rituals that resemble church services. One way to make the spirits come is to sacrifice animals to them, which has not endeared them to animal-rights groups. Santeríans try not to attract much attention, although their shops selling charms, herbs, potions, and ornaments associated with voodoo are familiar sights in Miami, Florida, and New York City.

Satanic Cults. Probably no cults are more notorious than the satanic ones. These cults are so unpopular in the public mind that they tend to go underground and recruit new members secretly. Books and television shows have given them extensive coverage and publicity. Whole communities have been torn apart by the belief that there were devil worshipers in their midst, corrupting their children and practicing obscene rituals in private homes.

Actually, there are very few satanic cults that have openly stated their beliefs and sought approval by the public. The first was the Church of Satan, founded in 1966 by Anton LaVey. Two of the books he wrote were *The Satanic Bible* in 1969 and *Satanic Rituals* in 1972. LaVey did not promote human sacrifice or sexual excess or any of the other rumored practices of satanists, but he took the opposite view of human conduct from that of established religions. He believed that pleasure is

*K*arla LaVey stands in front of a life-size wax statue of her late father, Anton LaVey, who founded the Church of Satan in 1966.

the guiding principle in life, and people should do whatever pleases them. Love for humankind did not enter into his thinking. If someone does you a bad turn, you should get even. If someone is poor or handicapped, he or she probably deserves it, so why waste your time on him or her. His approach did not prove popular, so he abandoned his church and communicated with believers through the mail until his death in 1997. Satanism, however, continues to be written about and talked about, and its very notoriety may be one of its greatest attractions to young or impressionable minds.

Cults from the East

The 1960s saw an increase in cultic activity due to the turmoil of the times. Civil rights conflicts, the assassinations of John F. and Robert Kennedy, Martin Luther King, Jr., and Malcolm X, and above all the Vietnam War caused many young people to question all of the values that were held by their elders. Many of them turned to beliefs and ideals that were as different from Western models as possible. The Far East offered such alternatives, and the nation seemed to be swamped with cults, sects, and new religions from India, China, and Japan.

Hare Krishna. The Hare Krishna cult was brought from India in 1965 by Swami Prabhupada, a Hindu religious teacher. He reported that he had a vision that told him to take his teaching to the West. He founded the International Society for Krishna Consciousness, which immediately attracted large numbers of white, middle-class young people. Members were required to leave their homes and settle in communes, take new names, and adopt the dress of religious students in India. Many went barefoot, wore long white or yellow gowns, and shaved their heads. Their main ritual was to attain a state of bliss or joy induced by a trance that was achieved by intense concentration and the chanting of "Hare Krishna, Hare Krishna." Cult members soon became a familiar sight in big cities, where they chanted and sold their publications in airplane terminals, railroad stations, and any other public place that could not put them out.

What alarmed people most about the Hare Krishnas was that they had somehow seduced a great many young people to leave their homes, families, and friends to devote their lives to an

A follower of Hare Krishna makes a call on his cell phone in front of the new Hare Krishna complex in New Delhi, India. Members claim that they are moving away from the fringes of society.

unfamiliar ritual. The parents of these converts were horrified, and many complained that their children had been virtually kidnapped. The Hare Krishnas didn't seem to be doing much harm, however, and they won approval in some circles. The cult strongly disapproved of the use of drugs, and many of their members who were drug users gave up their habit at the insistence of the cult.

The Hare Krishnas continued to gain new members during the 1970s and began to make money through the sale of their publications, incense, and vegetarian foods. They became more aggressive in their recruiting and in their public appeals for funds. People began to be annoyed by their chanting and strange looks and behavior. Some cult members went back to their old ways and began to smuggle drugs into the country. When parents tried to legally get their children back, the cult would transfer the teenagers from one of their communes to another to keep them away from the authorities.

The Hare Krishnas became increasingly aggressive and even violent. In October 1985 the leader of one of their communes was shot by one of his followers. Then, in 1990, two more commune leaders were accused of illegal fund-raising and one was found guilty. In 1991, a federal investigation of the organization led to charges of arson, rack-eteering, and conspiracy. The bad publicity ruined their recruiting efforts, and many members began leaving the cult. Hare Krishna, which was once one of the largest and most noticeable cults in the United States, now has fewer than five thousand members, and its activity in public places has virtually ceased.

The Divine Light Mission. Another cult imported from India is the Divine Light Mission, which attracted many followers in the late 1960s. It, too, was charged with brainwashing and abduction of minors and soon fell into disrepute. Part of this was due to the erratic behavior of its teenage leader, Maharaj Ji. He had brought the cult to America against the advice of his family, which had founded the cult in India. Maharaj Ji, at sixteen, married his twenty-four-year-old secretary and soon lost the respect of his followers. He engaged in nasty legal fights with his family over leadership of the cult, which further damaged his image. In 1980, Maharaj Ji changed the name of the cult to Elan Vital, but was unable to recapture his following. Now he is seldom heard from.

The Rajneesh Foundation International. **Another** cult from India, the Rajneesh Foundation International, attracted a great deal of attention in the early 1990s because of its political activities. Bhagwan (godman) Rajneesh, who was a religious instructor in Jainism, founded it in India in 1966. The followers of Jainism believe in reincarnation and follow a simple life apart from what they consider the sinful world. Rajneesh did not believe that it was necessary to withdraw from the world in order to lead a holy life, and he attracted enough followers to establish a commune. When the commune was destroyed by fire in 1981, he and his followers moved to the United States.

Rajneesh tried to reestablish his commune in Antelope, Oregon, and promptly ran into trouble. He purchased sixty-four thousand acres of land and announced his plan to build a community to house his followers. The people of Oregon did not want a huge community built in the middle of their beautiful forests and streams. Environmentalists and landowners started a campaign against the cult. The Rajneesh Foundation began to build their community and requested that they be allowed to become part of the town of Antelope rather than a separate community just for cult members. The town agreed, and the cult members promptly began to run for office. Since they outnumbered the longtime citizens of Antelope, they easily won election to important posts, and one of them even became mayor. The cult's power play was eventually stopped when immigration officials found out that many of the members, including Rajneesh, had entered the country illegally. He was deported, the land was sold, and the cult broke up into several small communities throughout the country.

The Nation of Islam. The Black Muslims were founded in Detroit, Michigan, but have an Eastern background, as can be seen in its formal name, the Nation of Islam. Its founder was Wallace D. Fard, who called himself the Supreme Ruler of the Universe. Fard's message to his followers was that black people were the original race of humans and had built the ancient city of Mecca, which is the spiritual center of the Nation of Islam located in what is now Saudi Arabia. White people were created by a mad scientist about six thousand years ago and had caused trouble to blacks ever since. Fard's aim was to unite African Americans against the white people and regain their true religion and status in the world.

Fard disappeared in 1934. No one knows where or why, or if they do, they are not saying. He was succeeded by Elijah Muhammad, who ran things quietly while enjoying a lavish lifestyle until Malcolm X began to challenge his leadership. Malcolm X (many Black Muslims put an X after their names to indicate that slavery had robbed them of their true names) was the head of the Harlem branch of the Nation of Islam, which was one of the largest and most important. Malcolm X urged his followers to turn away from all "white man's" religions, especially Christianity, which continued to enslave blacks by "brainwashing" them. He regularly referred to white people as "white devils" and threatened violence against them if he did not achieve his goals. He called for a separate homeland for African Americans, although he never gave any idea of how this could be brought about. His radicalism soon began to alarm Black Muslim

Profile of a Cult

✓ Female members 64%

✓ Male members............................. 36%

✓ Married members 41%

✓ Single members 36%

✓ Divorced members 19%

✓ Separated members........................ 4%

✓ Average age at joining cult................. 24.8

✓ Average number of years
belonging to cult........................... 6.7

✓ Average number of years of schooling
before joining.............................. 13.4

Religious affiliation before joining cult:

✓ Protestant................................. 47%

✓ Catholic.................................. 24%

✓ Jewish..................................... 8%

✓ None...................................... 13%

✓ Other..................................... 8%

Source: Preliminary report on the "Questionnaire
for Former Members of Charismatic Groups"
prepared by Michael D. Langone, Ph.D., for
Cultic Studies Journal, American Family
Foundation, Bonita Springs, FL 34133,
July 20, 1992.

leaders as well as white people, and they began to openly oppose him. Malcolm X resigned from the Black Muslims—some people say he was expelled—and formed his own organization called the Muslim Mosque. He began to speak out against Black Muslims as well as whites, until he was assassinated in February 1965.

Malcolm X was succeeded by Louis Farrakhan, who also spoke out against all white people in general and Jews in particular. He did not, however, call for a separate homeland for African Americans. His hatred and bigotry became softened somewhat in the 1990s, and he has begun to consider peaceful means to improve the lives of his followers. In October 1995 he organized the "Million Man March" to demonstrate African-American men's solidarity. The march was a success, but it did little to improve his standing with the public, since he began immediately to seek support from the United States' bitterest political enemies in Libya and Iraq.

Nondestructive Cults

While many cults prepare for doomsday or try to separate themselves from what they perceive as sinful mankind or preach hate and bigotry, there have always been cults that promote love and peace and try to establish a heavenly paradise on earth. These are the utopian cults, which flourished in the nineteenth century, and the New Age cults, which have recently sprung up in the later part of the twentieth century.

Utopian cults take their name from the book *Utopia* (1516) by Thomas More, which described an imaginary, perfect country in which happiness was finally achieved by all its inhabitants. Members of utopian cults try to live perfect lives of peace and harmony. They are usually self-supporting, sharing their worldly goods with one another. They tend to live apart in communities and usually depend upon a strong leader to see them through the opposition they are bound to encounter from the outside world. These leaders usually claim that they found their mission in life through visions. The Shakers, the Mormons, and the Oneida are probably the best known of the nineteenth-century utopian cults, and they have all grown into respectful and respected parts of American society. The Mormons, of course, have been the most successful and have become one of America's established religions.

The Shakers. The Shakers were one of America's earliest cults, dating from 1774, just before the Revolutionary War. They got their name from the fact that their members would begin to tremble and shake when they felt a vision coming on during their religious meetings. Their founder, Anna Lee, established communities throughout New York State and New England. She was against violence of any sort, which led her to denounce the Revolutionary War and to accuse the rebels of sinfulness. The Shakers were never very popular with the American patriots after that. They survived all attempts to force them to abandon their beliefs, however, and they established communities in which they lived quiet and peaceful lives. They practiced sexual abstinence and were careful about admitting new members to their meetings. People began to admire their plain and simple lives, especially as reflected in their dress, household goods, and furniture that was so perfectly designed that it is still popular today.

The Mormons. The Church of Jesus Christ of

Latter Day Saints is the formal name for the Mormon Church. It was founded by Joseph Smith, Jr., in Palmyra, New York, in 1830. Smith claimed to have visions of Jesus Christ, who urged him to form his own church since all existing churches were corrupt. He also said that he had a vision of an angel named Moroni, who told him of the history of the earliest peoples of the North American continent. These were descended from the ancient tribes of Israel. Their history could be found on metal plates buried nearby. Smith claimed to have dug up the plates and published them as *The Book of Mormon.* Smith was a forceful preacher, and he soon had a number of followers. He maintained strict control over his group and its beliefs. He moved his headquarters to Kirkland, Ohio, in 1831, and sent out missionaries to gain converts to what he claimed was a new religion. The Mormons were an aloof society that had their own economy. Their neighbors distrusted them, and they were discriminated against wherever they went. They were forced to move their headquarters to Nauvoo, Illinois, in 1839.

Smith continued to have visions and receive instructions from his angelic visitors. He claimed that he was ordered by God to have more than one wife. When some of his followers objected to this, Smith ordered that all the church's elders, or officials, also take many wives. Some of his followers expressed their disagreement with Smith and denounced him in their newspaper. He and his brother destroyed the newspaper, and as a result they were put into prison. An angry mob of followers and neighbors later broke into the prison and killed Smith and his brother.

How People Become Attracted to Cults

✓ Through a friend who joined a group 34%

✓ Through a boyfriend or girlfriend
  who joined a group 25%

✓ Through a brother or sister
  who joined a group 23%

✓ Through reading materials. 20%

✓ Through a recruiter on a college campus 11%

✓ Through a meeting on a street
  (not on campus) 13%

✓ Other 33%

Note: *Some subjects checked more than one item, so total is greater than 100%.*

Source: Preliminary report on the "Questionnaire for Former Members of Charismatic Groups," prepared by Michael D. Langone, Ph.D., for *Cultic Studies Journal*, American Family Foundation, Bonita Springs, FL 34133, July 20, 1992.

Smith was succeeded by Brigham Young, who moved the church to Utah. Brigham Young also had many wives, and he ordered that all Mormon men should take more than one wife. This got him into trouble with the United States government, which had passed laws against multiple marriages. These laws blocked Utah's chances for admission into the United States until the church finally did away with the doctrine of many wives in 1890. By this time, the Mormons had firmly established themselves in Utah and had gained followers throughout the country and in Europe. The church gradually lost its cult-like traits, and over the years became accepted as part of American society. Today it is one of America's major religious denominations and claims to have more than 3 million members throughout the world.

Oneida. The Oneida cult grew out of the idea of its founder, John Humphrey Noyes, that anything he did, as long as it was meant well, was all right with God. What Noyes liked to do was make love to women, but his marriage vows prevented him from doing freely what he most liked to do. So in 1848 he gathered about him several couples who agreed secretly to practice "free love," as it was then called. This soon got him into trouble with the law, so he left his home in Vermont and set up a community in Oneida, New York, where his followers could have complete sexual freedom. Noyes dictated the sexual practices of his followers and otherwise controlled their lives. He did this, he said, in order to establish a paradise on earth. His followers might have had fun for a while, but they soon became bored and restless. The young people of the community, who were not so sure that Oneida was paradise, wanted to grow up and have lives of their own. The people in the surrounding communities finally became fed up with the goings-on at Oneida and threatened Noyes with adultery and rape charges. He fled to Canada, leaving his eldest son in charge of the community. However, the son did not have his father's flare for organizing other people's lives. Members of the community soon began to drift away or settled down as citizens of upstate New York. In 1881, another of Noyes's sons set up a business community, one of whose products was sterling-silver tableware. Oneida silverware, which is still manufactured and sold today, is one of America's finest trademarks.

Spiritual Cults

While utopians sought to find their goal of paradise in this world, spiritual cults looked to the other world for guidance. Many people, especially primitive peoples, believe in spirits of the dead who can control life on earth. Many cults have been formed by people, called mediums, who claim to make contact with the dead while in a trance. Mediums have been active throughout recorded history, from ancient Greece to medieval Japan. One of the most famous spiritual cults, because of its historical importance, was the Ghost Dance cult of the western Plains Indians.

The Ghost Dance. Around 1870, a Paiute Indian prophet named Wovoka had visions in which he was taken up into the land of the dead and given directions on how to achieve happiness and peace on earth. The ritual consisted of a dance that could last for days in which the participants worked themselves into such a frenzy that they could communicate with the spirits of the dead. As the Ghost Dance spread from tribe to tribe throughout the Great Plains area, the dances became larger and more elaborate. To the white settlers of Wisconsin and Minnesota, these dances seemed more like war dances in which the Indians were

The Oldest Existing Cult in the World

The Assassins are a secret order of religious fanatics founded in Iran in the eleventh century by the Persian Hasan al-Sabbah. Hasan and later leaders of the cult were each known as "The Old Man of the Mountain." Members of the cult were known for their blind obedience to their leader and considered the murder of their enemies a sacred duty. Their name comes from the Arabic word *hashshashin*, or addicts of the drug hashish, which they used to induce visions of paradise. They believed that in following the secret rites of the group, they would receive hidden power and timeless wisdom. They were rewarded by being given a glimpse of paradise on earth, which in reality was a secret pleasure garden hidden in the mountains of northern Syria. They were known to the early Italian trader Marco Polo, who visited their secret pleasure garden in 1271, and to the Christian crusaders, against whom they conducted a fearful campaign of murder and assassination. They were eventually defeated by the Mongols and Egyptians in the thirteenth century, and their members were scattered throughout Asia Minor and India. The cult exists today in scattered groups of various names located in northern Syria, Iran, Zanzibar, Oman, and India.

working themselves into a frenzy before attacking the white settlements. The alarmed settlers called in the army, which arrested the leader of the Sioux Indians, Sitting Bull. A conflict followed in which Sitting Bull and several army officers were killed. This led to the final tragedy at Wounded Knee Reservation, when through a series of misunderstandings, violence broke out and more than two hundred Indians were killed. This put an end to the Ghost Dance cult but prolonged the Indian wars that were to bring so much violence and hardship to the western states.

Theosophists. Spiritualism traveled east and was revived in New England with the foundation of the cult of Theosophy. The word *theosophy* comes from two Greek words: *theo*, meaning "God," and *sophia*, meaning "wisdom" or "knowledge." This cult was started by Madame Helena Petrovna Blavatsky, a medium from Russia who claimed to have contact with the spirit world. She took her knowledge and techniques from religious leaders in India called gurus, who were supposed to be inhabited by wise spirits of the dead. The goal of all her study and experiments in trances and visions was, as usual with spiritualist cults, an earthly paradise, or a New Age, in which people were kind and good and evil was expelled. Few people argued with her intentions, but Madame Blavatsky was constantly being exposed as a fraud in the press. Nevertheless, her influence continued even after her death in 1891. Most of the New Age cults can be traced to the influence of the Theosophist Society, as Madame Blavatsky's cult was named.

New Age Cults

New Age cults began in the 1970s at the height of the hippie movement, when people congregated in San Francisco, sang folk songs, practiced free love, wore flowers in their hair, and demonstrated against what they felt were military and corporate wrongdoings. The New Agers were helped by the publication of best-selling books in which ordinary people claimed to have experienced gorgeous past lives. Madame Blavatsky's technique for contacting the spirit world was called "channeling," and New Agers everywhere began to become possessed by wise spirits who directed others to become kind and good. To help channelers connect with the spirit world, New Age cults offered all sorts of tools such as Tarot cards, potions, herbs, lotions, spells, and reading material ranging from street handouts to glossy magazines and books. All these were available in shops in every large city across the country. The problem with the New Age cults was that hardly anyone took them seriously. They became the target of jokes and comic skits on television. The popular opinion was that they were all "airheads." When their efforts did nothing to change the world, the members themselves began to lose heart. They still exist, but mostly as owners of quaint little shops selling the worn-out tools of Madame Blavatsky.

Scientology

The Church of Scientology, on the other hand, has thrived. It was started in 1950 by a science-fiction writer named L. Ron Hubbard. It can be defined as a spiritualist cult because Hubbard claimed to be in touch with a whole empire of spirits that had been cast out of the world 75 million years ago.

Hubbard's message was very complicated, but basically it had to do with "clearing" oneself of negative feelings and tendencies one had inherited from previous lives. The way to get rid of these negative influences and achieve happiness was to undergo therapy under the direction of an "auditor," or listener. The troubled person seeking this therapy was encouraged to speak into a machine that resembled a lie detector. The auditor, of course, listened and determined what could be done to help the speaker. This whole program of "clearing" was very expensive, but many people seemed willing to pay to have themselves purified. In fact, the Church of Scientology is primarily a money-making enterprise that resembles a large corporation—modern high-rise buildings, private retreats, private yachts and airplanes, foreign offices, public relations and advertising departments, and a large publishing division. It has been helped in its public image by the endorsement of celebrities such as John Travolta, Tom Cruise, Lisa-Marie Presley, Kirstie Alley, and the late Sonny Bono.[2] It has been attacked constantly from the outside by every responsible newspaper, magazine, publisher, or broadcaster and by former members who have defected. The cult, following the practice of its founder while he was alive, has responded by counterattacking every charge. In any given year, it has hundreds of lawsuits pending in every state and abroad, and it is said that it employs more than one hundred lawyers to whom it pays an estimated $20 million each year.[3] Scientology appears to be with us to stay, and, who knows, some day it may attain the status of a real church.

Mr. Travolta

*A*ctor John Travolta (left) looks on as singer Chick Corea testifies on Capitol Hill in 1997 before the Helsinki Commission hearing about discrimination against Scientologists in Germany.

Space-age Cults

One type of cult that could only have happened in the twentieth century is based on outer-space phenomena. These cults are called by different names—UFO cults, flying-saucer cults, extra-terrestrial cults—but they all are centered on the belief that beings from outer space or other galaxies control our lives and destinies. Some of the leaders of these cults claim to have been abducted by extraterrestrials. They say that they were taken up in spaceships and given special knowledge of the past and future by their abductors. Some cults in other categories have taken on some of the beliefs of the outer-space cults. Heaven's Gate, for example, believed that a spaceship following the Hale-Bopp comet of 1997 would whisk them aboard once they had freed themselves from their earthly lives.[4] L. Ron Hubbard, the founder of the Church of Scientology, claimed to have had many experiences and revelations from and in outer space. New as they may be, however, these space-age cults still have the basic characteristics of most cults. Their leaders have a special knowledge or calling, although in their case it comes from extraterrestrial contacts or revelations. Their followers consider themselves special because only they know the truth.

Chapter 5

Cults Among Us

Many people find it strange that members of a cult turn their backs on what society thinks important. Cult members seem to have no use for what most of us think of as right or true or sacred. How could this happen? Who are these people who become members of cults?

Cult Members

Cults have traditionally drawn their members from adolescents or young adults, people who may be in that stage of life when confusion and uncertainty seems to accompany any action or belief. An intense personal problem, such as an argument with parents or a failed romantic attachment, or a tragic public event, such as an assassination or a riot, may cause a person to question the whole value system of the society in which he or she is supposed to participate.

Cult recruiters realize that the teen years are a time of uncertainty and that many young people are looking for direction. Cults are only too happy to supply that direction. Their recruiters often center their efforts on college campuses, where many young people are away from home for the first time. Many students join cults out of curiosity or because others are doing it or just for the companionship that cults seem to offer. Many lonely people have been drawn into a cult simply because its members seemed to welcome their company.

Cults focus on young people because they hope that they can attract other young people, provide the hard work that may be involved in maintaining a separate community, or even that they may grow up in the cult, marry, and have children who will remain loyal to the cult. The only problem with a cult composed mostly of young people, however, is that they cannot supply money or income to the group. That is why cults are increasingly trying to recruit older people as a source of funds.

Older people can be plagued by as much doubt and uncertainty as teenagers. The loss of a job may cause feelings of unworthiness. A divorce can cause loneliness or loss of direction in life. The transition from youth to middle and old age can cause depression or anxiety. Researchers have noticed that cults are turning to recruiting people, especially women, who are experiencing midlife crises. Retirees are also desirable cult members, since many of them have saved considerable funds for their retirement, which they can contribute to the group. Many retirees are easy to recruit, since they have worked all their lives and feel lost without a specific purpose in their days. A cult will readily supply a reason to live for elderly people.

Whatever their reasons for joining, most cult members seem unaware of some of the consequences of cult membership. Cults must have money to survive and spread their message for good

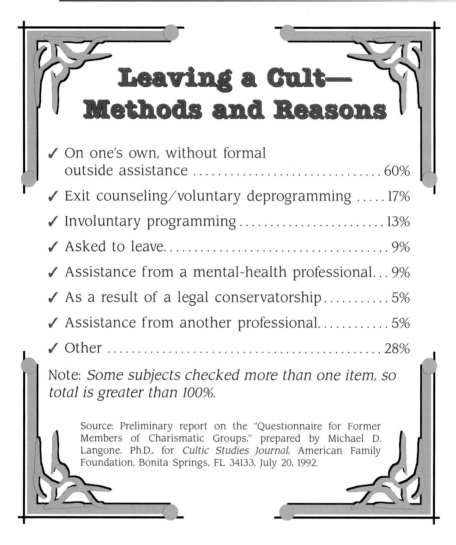

Leaving a Cult—Methods and Reasons

✓ On one's own, without formal
  outside assistance 60%

✓ Exit counseling/voluntary deprogramming 17%

✓ Involuntary programming 13%

✓ Asked to leave................................... 9%

✓ Assistance from a mental-health professional... 9%

✓ As a result of a legal conservatorship........... 5%

✓ Assistance from another professional............ 5%

✓ Other 28%

Note: *Some subjects checked more than one item, so total is greater than 100%.*

Source: Preliminary report on the "Questionnaire for Former Members of Charismatic Groups," prepared by Michael D. Langone, Ph.D., for *Cultic Studies Journal*, American Family Foundation, Bonita Springs, FL 34133, July 20, 1992.

or ill. Most of their money comes from members, but if this is not enough, they must engage in moneymaking enterprises that are staffed by cult members. Some cults, such as the Hare Krishnas, turn their members into virtual beggars. Some make their members work at menial jobs with little or no pay, and the results of their labor go to the cult. Other cults engage in fraudulent and even illegal practices, which can result in jail sentences or fines for cult members. Scientologists, Moonies, Rajneesh Internationals, and many others have been found guilty in court of civil crimes. But the worst consequence of cult membership can be injury, death, suicide, and murder, as happened with Heaven's Gate, the People's Temple, the Manson family, the Branch Davidians, and many more. This alone should make any reasonable person suspicious and distrusting of cults.

Anticult Movements

As might be expected, many people began to investigate, expose, and accuse cults of destructive behavior. The parents of young people recruited by cults were the first and most concerned, as were relatives and friends of the victims of suicide and murderous cults. As public awareness of cults and their negative characteristics grew, people began to organize against them. At first these organizations were local and concerned with cults in their immediate neighborhoods or towns. Eventually national organizations began to appear, such as the Christian Research Institute, which were mostly concerned about religious cults and the inroads they made on established Christianity. Anticultism began to spread in the 1970s and new groups appeared who were more worried about the social and cultural impact of cults. Many of these groups merged into what became known as the Cult Awareness Network (CAN). CAN established an education program that exposed all the destructive characteristics of cults. Its members campaigned widely in print and on television, and the general public for the large part agreed with their message: Cults were destructive

*E*ighty-one people, including cult leader David Koresh, died in the fire that destroyed the Branch Davidian compound near Waco, Texas, on April 19, 1993.

and dangerous, said CAN, and clearly violate "our laws, our ethics, and our morals."[1]

Cult members were quick to respond. The larger and more affluent ones, particularly the Church of Scientology, started education programs of their own. They charged that anticultists were discriminating against minority religions. A more serious charge was that anticultists were violating the civil rights of cult members by preventing them from the free exercise of their beliefs. This charge came about because one of the anticultists' objectives was to "deprogram" cult members.

A father who was alarmed by his son's involvement in a cult called Children of God became an outright opponent of all cults. Ted Patrick, one of the founders of FREECOG (Free Our Children from the Children of God) believed that cults actually hypnotized recruits and then brainwashed them into becoming willing slaves to their leaders. He carried things a bit too far, however, by actually kidnapping cult members and submitting them to a deprogramming ritual that was almost as bad as anything he accused the cults of doing. Worse, he began selling his services to parents who wanted their children back. He soon lost the confidence of most people concerned with the destructiveness of cults,[2] and anticult activity has since been devoted largely to educational programs.

Anticultists have attempted to have legislation passed by state governments to prohibit cult activity, but they have failed. The United States Constitution absolutely forbids any restriction on thought or belief, so any attempt to curb the growth or continuation of cults is fruitless. Cultists insist that their groups are no different from the Masons, the Elks, the Rotary Clubs, and other organizations that have banded together for their own entertainment or satisfaction and for the public good. Unfortunately, the only time that cults can be brought to attention or accountability is when disaster strikes in the form of illegal acts, such as murder and suicide.

Cults have their defenders, but none has justified the practices and activities that have led to tragic consequences. They tend to blame these tragedies on extreme law enforcement tactics or on prejudiced outsiders who cannot understand their mission. The greatest critics of cults, however, are former cult members, who have charged their groups of everything from fraud and extortion to sexual abuse and torture. Many organizations exist to help former cult members readjust to mainstream life. That they exist at all, anticultists argue, is evidence that something is basically wrong with cults.

Cults and the Law

Anticultists have attempted to use legal and political means to curb the influence of cults. At first they tried to have courts grant special powers, called conservatorships, to parents whose children were members of cults. This would give parents the right to make legal decisions for their children even if the children were adults. The courts have usually denied them these powers, since it would deny freedom of choice. The courts' position has been that cult members joined of their own free will and unless they were being criminally held against their will, they could not be touched. Anticultists then turned to government for help, urging their representatives to introduce legislation barring cults or making them illegal. Although hearings and investigations of cults occurred in some states, nothing of any consequence has been done.

Cultists responded with lawsuits of their own, and since their stance was on freedom of religion and expression, they received sympathetic treatment from the courts. The Church of Scientology has been so active in suing anticult organizations that they have forced some into bankruptcy, including CAN, and effectively silenced others.[3] (CAN is now owned and operated by the Church of Scientology.) However, the battle still goes on, and, if nothing else, it has kept the matter of cults in the public eye. Every incidence of cult disruptiveness and tragedy, such as that of the Branch Davidians and Heaven's Gate, is given front-page and prime-time treatment. This cannot improve the public opinion of cults in our society. Many cults are, after all, secret organizations, and any exposure to public scrutiny is more likely to hurt them than win acceptance for them. This seems to be the current thrust of anticult activity: education of the public and exposure of the cults.

Cults in Cyberspace

After the mass suicide of the members of Heaven's Gate, an investigation of their activities revealed that they had discovered and used a new and effective way to recruit members. It was cyberspace and the Internet. They derived most of their operating funds from their work designing Web site pages for corporate and private companies. All the members, it appeared, were skilled computer operators, and they invaded the Internet in a thorough and methodical manner. They posted broadcasts to news groups. They chatted with teenagers, and they had their own Web site, which one commentator said must qualify as the most elaborate suicide note in history.[4]

Once it was discovered that the Internet had been used by Heaven's Gate, it did not take long to find other cults with their own Web sites, chat groups, and news services. Most parents received this news with dismay. Here was one more outside influence on their children over which they had little or no control. Anticultists soon responded to the challenge and established their own Web sites, news groups, and information exchanges. Like so

Degree of Difficulty in Leaving the Cult

✓ Very difficult 47%

✓ Difficult 25%

✓ Mildly difficult 11%

✓ No difficulty 14%

✓ Not sure 4%

Note: *Some subjects checked more than one item, so total is greater than 100%.*

Source: Preliminary report on the "Questionnaire for Former Members of Charismatic Groups," prepared by Michael D. Langone, Ph.D., for *Cultic Studies Journal*, American Family Foundation, Bonita Springs, FL 34133, July 20, 1992.

much about the Internet, no one seems to know what is permissible and what is destructive. Since many children know much more about computers than their parents do, it seems pointless to install a screening device like those that attempt to filter out pornographic Web sites. Any competent computer operator can soon discover ways to bypass such controls.

So the battle goes on between the cults and the anticultists, waged in print, the airwaves, and cyberspace. Because of our laws that jealously guard the rights of free speech, worship, and thought, the cults seem to have legal protection. The anticultists, however, have made significant advances by focusing on education and exposure. The cults have the laws on their side, but the anticultists seem to have public opinion on theirs. For the average person, a demand or even a request that he or she give up all worldly goods, swear devotion to a leader or an idea, work unceasingly and with little or no pay, and perhaps even agree to kill someone else or himself or herself on the order of the leader would seem to be insane. On the other hand, for someone who professes to know the truth or to believe in one who does, the duties and demands of cult membership, no matter how outrageous, may make sense.

American Family Foundation
P.O. Box 413005, Suite 313
Naples, FL 34101-3005
(941) 514-3081
<http://www.csj.org/>

Christian Research Institute
P.O. Box 7000
Rancho Santa Margarita, CA 92688-7000
(949) 858-6100
<http://www.equip.org/index.html>

Cult Clinic & Hot Line
Jewish Board of Child and Family Services
120 West Fifty-seventh Street
New York, NY 10019
(212) 632-4640

InfoCult
5655 Park Avenue
Montreal, Quebec
Canada H2V 4H2
(514) 274-2333

Any of these organizations or services can be contacted to locate any organization in a specific locale or with a special interest.

Chapter 1. Cults in the News

1. Elizabeth Gleick, "The Marker We've Been . . . Waiting For," *Time*, April 7, 1997, p. 28.

2. George Klineman and Sherman Butler, *The Cult That Died: The Tragedy of Jim Jones and the Peoples Temple* (New York: G. P. Putnam's Sons, 1980), p. 359.

3. Steven Butler, "Chasing Down the Cultists," *U.S. News and World Report*, May 29, 1995, p. 42.

4. Michael D. Langone, "Clinical Update on Cults," *Psychiatric Times*, July 1996, p. 14.

Chapter 2. What Is a Cult?

1. Margaret Thaler Singer with Janja Lalich, *Cults in Our Midst* (San Francisco: Jossey-Bass Publishers, 1995), pp. 6–9.

2. Elizabeth Gleick, "The Marker We've Been . . . Waiting For," *Time*, April 7, 1997, pp. 28–36.

3. James D. Tabor and Eugene V. Gallagher, *Why Waco?: Cults and the Battle for Religious Freedom in America* (Berkeley and Los Angeles, Calif.: University of California Press, 1995), p. 152.

Chapter 3. Where Do Cults Come From?

1. Robert C. Solomon and Kathleen M. Higgens, *A Short History of Philosophy* (New York: Oxford University Press, 1996), pp. 27–28.

2. Margaret Thaler Singer with Janja Lalich, *Cults in Our Midst* (San Francisco: Jossey-Bass Publishers, 1995), p. 29.

3. Alan Cooperman, "The Same Could Happen Here," *U.S. News & World Report*, April 3, 1995, p. 36.

Chapter 4. What Kinds of Cults Are There?

1. Kay Marie Porterfield, *Straight Talk About Cults* (New York: Facts On File, Inc., 1955), p. 102.

2. Richard Behar, "The Thriving Cult of Greed and Power," *Time*, May 6, 1991, p. 50.

3. Ibid., p. 56.

4. Elizabeth Gleick, "The Marker We've Been . . . Waiting For," *Time*, April 7, 1997, pp. 28–36.

Chapter 5. Cults Among Us

1. James D. Tabor and Eugene V. Gallagher, *Why Waco?: Cults and the Battle for Religious Freedom in America* (Berkeley and Los Angeles, Calif.: University of California Press, 1995), p. 171.

2. Margaret Thaler Singer with Janja Lalich, *Cults in Our Midst* (San Francisco: Jossey-Bass Publishers, 1995), pp. 284–285.

3. Frank Rich, "Who Can Stand Up? (To Scientology)," *The New York Times*, March 16, 1997, p. A19.

4. Joshua Quittner, "Life and Death on the Web," *Time*, April 7, 1997, p. 47.

Appel, Willa. *Cults in America: Programmed for Paradise*. New York: Holt, Rinehart and Winston, 1981.

Barghusen, Joan D. *Cults*. San Diego: Lucent Books, 1997.

Hexham, Irving, and Karla Poewe. *Understanding Cults and New Religions*. Grand Rapids, Mich.: Wm. B. Eerdmans Publishing Co., 1986.

Porterfield, Kay Marie. *Straight Talk About Cults*. New York: Facts On File, Inc., 1995.

Singer, Margaret Thaler, with Janja Lalich. *Cults in Our Midst*. San Francisco: Jossey-Bass Publishers, 1995.

Tabor, James D., and Eugene V. Gallagher. *Why Waco?: Cults and the Battle for Religious Freedom in America*. Berkeley and Los Angeles, Calif.: University of California Press, 1995.

Zeinert, Karen. *Cults*. Springfield, N.J.: Enslow Publishers, Inc. 1997.

Further Reading